Keep Those Clients

Learn Relationship Marketing, Double Your Business & Get Endless Referrals

By Laurie Delk

What is Relationship Marketing, and how do I do it?

Relationship Marketing, is a facet of Customer Relationship Management (CRM) focusing on customer loyalty and long-term customer engagement rather than short-term goals like customer acquisition and individual sales. It is a management strategy designed to encourage strong and lasting connections to your brand, service or product. The goal is to turn your prospects into loyal customers who will then generate repeat sales, and encourage and give word-of-mouth promotions (referrals).

Yes, the goal is create loyal, long-term referring customers! I say this with humility, as many of us should bring a bit of humility to our business, and let go of expectations. Be respectful of yourself and your customers/clients, referrals, and potential clients. Don't force people into "liking you." Value your message because you value yourself as the messenger. The value you place in yourself as the messenger is the confidence you need to take the necessary steps outlined in this book.

You may be thinking, "I don't own my own business. I work for someone else." Well, then, this information is still for you. Even if you are "working in someone else's business, we better ourselves, our personal business/sales, when we live and believe we are working for ourselves. If you are a sales person, account representative, working on commission, etc … know and understand this … you are working for yourself. Your effort directly effects your result (income).

You will get out of a relationship what you put into the relationship.

When I started my web and graphic design business, back in 1994, my Dad told me, "Never mix business with personal and never mix business with religion". Back then, he was right, maybe. ☺ But now-a-days, that is not so. Now-a-days people are craving relationships. Maybe it has something to do with so many hiding behind the computer screen, their phones, etc. We need that extra something when it comes to human contact.

People want to know who you are, they want to see the *real* you. We all struggle, at some point in our lives with a specific question, "Where do I fit in?" It is our relationships ... it is who we have relationships with ... that tells us exactly where we fit into this crazy world.

Building a Relationship

Relationships all start in the same place. Two strangers meeting and desire to get to know each other. Sometimes there are sparks in the beginning; sometimes the relationship requires time. Building a relationship requires 2 people to show and be who they are. Building a true relationship is about letting the authentic you shine through. Building a quality relationship requires your heart to lead you, the wall must come down. When our wall comes down, the other person in the relationship can and will feel comfortable letting their wall down as well. We are sharing a story and creating a new part of the story together.

Isolation doesn't build anything but loneliness.

So, the question is, how does the wall come "tumbling down"?

"You don't build a business. You build people and then you build a business."
- Zig Ziglar

As you are building your relationships, and as you network, you grow your contact list:

1. Seek to truly understand the person.

2. When you understand the person, you can make them feel more comfortable more easily.

3. Don't over complicate the relationship or the relationship process.

4. Keep YOUR promises!

5. Be intentional in everything you do. In your words and in your actions.

6. We have all heard the saying, "Big things come in small packages." Well, the same in a relationship. Sometimes the smallest gift leave the largest impact!

One of the ways I let my heart and authentic "me" shine through is cards! I have always sent out cards, for everything. Think about a rose for a moment. The petals are all wrapped tightly in the beginning. Slowly, a petal opens. With each petal that opens a new picture is created. Something beautiful happens. All the petals are open; the rose is in full bloom. And, inside that bloom, we find the seeds. The seeds of life. Cards, for me, are the seeds of life. Sharing moments with my friends, my prospects, my clients are the petals slowly opening. Each card develops a deeper meaning ... until one day the picture is complete. Yes, I send cards to celebrate and share all occasions: Thank you for your business, nice to meet you, thank you for talking to me, birthday, Christmas, anniversary, etc. This is how I built a six-figure business, sitting at home, behind a computer, while nursing babies. ☺

It is a life for which most of us strive. Getting to be a part of our family while doing business. How can you get there, too? You can!

When you think of where your relationships are currently, create a strategy around these questions: How many are in the honeymoon phase? Which ones are in the new customer phase? Who are loyal? What are you doing to continue to build your relationships?

At the beginning of "my career", I never took any personal development courses. Although years later, I realized my Mom showed me as well as taught me much in her daily life of bringing up my sisters and I all along. What I did find as I grew in my life and in my business, I learned from every possible source. It was as if a lightbulb went off in my head and in my heart. There was still so much to learn. We have all thought or said, in some form or fashion, "I'm doing so good! I am rocking it out." We don't see where or what we can improve. But I did it in my life, and as I grew in my business, I did see where I could improve and what I had to do extraordinary every time I provided a service. As my business grew, I learned other things, and of course then I started buying all the books and audio books I could get my hands on for personal development and business success. The amazing thing I noticed almost all of the books/audiobooks, talk about building relationships with people and keeping in touch, and sending the handwritten note!

Want to find major success in life and in business? Get off of autopilot. Most business professionals are living on autopilot. Only doing what must be done. Remember this: 80% relationship building, and 20% marketing. This statement is power and life changing.

Be the light in someone's life. You never know what it could mean or where the light will lead you. One of my mentors, Kody Bateman: CEO Send Out Cards, showed me, plus I have learned over the years. Now, I have had the opportunity to have taught several business owners in different industries to implement, and in turn, they have found major success in their business! Again, the key in business is 80% relationship building and 20% marketing.

Have you ever thought about the definition of "relationship"? According to Merriam Webster the definition of relationship is: the way in which two or more people, groups, countries, etc., talk to, behave toward, and deal with each other or the way in which two or more people or things are connected.

The purpose of the relationship is to connect with someone else. How have you been connecting? Is it working effectively? Want it to work better? Let the story of you heart and the story of your service overcome the "marketing difficulties" the world tells us to see. Show your face to your prospects and clients. Be who you are. If you are an extrovert, let that abundance of love express itself. And, if you are an introvert, embrace the willingness to get to know someone at a core level without the "fluff." They will see how just how amazing you are!

This is the reason why we network. The reason why we attend events and put ourselves out there in the spotlight. Networking is simply connecting, linking, or working to operate interactively. When we connect, the people we are connecting with ... we must make it interactive. And, the best way to make it interactive is to follow up, provide quality service, and create the relationship.

In every interaction you have with your customer or client, 80% of your interactions should be relationship building. If you are always just trying to *sell* your customer, what will they think? What will their understanding of you be? All they think is they are a dollar sign to you. You must show your prospect and your clients/customers you are not just about the money. You are sharing with them you aren't someone who can be bought with a price.

Take the lead in the relationship. Never wait for someone else to reach out first. (If they do ... BONUS!) You take the lead with those 80% of interactions. Those interactions are ready willing and able to say, "I am the person who is about smiles, dancing, and celebrating with you!" Those 80% of interactions are bringing hope, encouragement, support, and hey, "I listen to you." The 80% of your connections, reach out's, are building something that will work for you. When you are building relationships with them, you are creating a strong and, even an emotional, connection to them. This connection leads to repeat business and even referrals (without you having to ask for them!). ☺

When you serve more than you expect, give more than you get, people become more than people you met.

When you connect with your customers and clients on social media (Facebook, linkedin, Instagram, etc), it can help you easily to monitor and respond to customer issues, if you have a business presence. And, maybe even more importantly, you can connect with them on a more personal level, if you have a personal account. For example, connecting on a personal level, as you see one of your clients, their child wins a soccer game and they post pictures about it, you can download those pictures, create a card for them, and send the card to the child telling them what a great job they did. Every child loves to get a special treat in the mail.

Something spectacular happens when there is a card, not a bill, in the mailbox. You just made a child happy, maybe you even made their week or month! How do you think that is going to make the parents feel about you? Do you think it might seal their connection with you, just a little more on a personal level? Of course it will! When you do that here and there on occasion, as well as doing good business, ethics etc, you are going to have your customers become your raving fans while giving you referrals without even asking. Your follow up and how your find the connection is still telling your story. You are becoming "greater" than your competition. And, just between you and me, you are creating an opportunity to be seen.

When you connect with the emotional side of your clients, especially in a positive way, you have turned the key to a long-term, happy relationship. Kindness draws people in! BAM! I would love to give you a high-five right now.

As Tom Hopkins says, **"People do business, with those they know, like and trust".**

Trust is a huge part of networking, relationships and marketing. Trust is one of the most powerful words. Trust is when you believe and other believe in your reliability and strength. Are you trustworthy? Do you customers/clients and potentials know that you are trustworthy? Connect and prove it to them!

What I have learned and now share, "They also refer others as well, and the ones they remember best, are the ones who are connecting with them often." They say you lose 10% influence with a client for every month you do not keep in touch with a client. So it is important to have a monthly *touch* with your clients. This can be in a variety of ways: texts, emails, phone calls, in person, greeting cards, gifts, and more. Just make sure you follow the 80% building the relationship and only 20% sales and marketing – and you will see the difference.

Why it works. You are nurturing your garden. For those of you who like to garden or even if you do not have a green thumb, taking care of your garden of customers and clients is an area where everyone can have a green thumb when they follow the 80/20 rule! You can be their water and their sunshine.

Alarming Statistics

- The #1 reason a customer doesn't come back is they simply forgot about you.

It doesn't matter what you sell or how great of a job you did – if they cannot find you when they need or want your service or product next. So, take care of your business. Not just the day-to-day, look to take care of your entire business ~ the people who make up your business.

Think of a window washer – You hire a window washer to wash the windows of your house maybe once every 6 months to a year. So a guy comes out, he does a great job; he is pleasant, well-mannered, seems ethical, honest, moral, good business and everything in his business is in line. But, in 6 months when you need him again, are you going to remember who you called? Are you going to remember where you put his business card? What about all the people within that 6 months with who you talked – how many times could you have referred his name out – IF he were *top of mind* in your thoughts?

The fact is, most people are going to lose or misplace your business card. Realistically, no one uses phone books any more. What are people doing instead? You know. Google! Or maybe you Yahoo. When your potential customer or client does a google or yahoo search, are you going to come up within the first 3-5 results? Hopefully so, but if not, and if you have not kept in touch, then you may lose that customer/client. They will find someone else because it is convenient. We live in a world based on convenience. What can we find on our phones ... we want everything to be held in our hands. The one thing you can always hold in your hand is the opportunity to reach out, the gratitude, the thank you, the experience of "I am here for you."

So, you must find your way to your clients'/customers' heart!

Idea for the window washer – Send out 5 cards a year – just personal, keep in touch, customized cards – birthday, anniversary, thank you for your business, hope you're having a great summer, and a Christmas card. Then, one marketing card. Keep it something that has to do with the window washing business such as tips for keeping windows cleaned in between visits, and then the window washer includes an offer to come do it. Cost is minimal – about $10. Think about this, service visits yield $200-500 so the window washer's ROI (return on investment) – just 1 extra service yields way more than the investment! Potential is many more service yields, plus referrals!

A simple keeping in touch campaign, can be done in many ways – emails, texts, greeting cards, connecting on social media, networking in person, etc. And, the best results come from using a mixture of all those.

- 95% of your happy customers, will purchase from a competitor on an impulse.

People have sales, ads, fliers, and all kinds of things confronting or distracting them every single day – radio, TV, music, social media, networking, all kinds of places. Many times people buy from your competitor just out of convenience. They happen to be right there when the person needs "that" certain item, and hey bonus, it's 20% off today too! A popular promo in business is and continues to be, "New Customer Promos." A huge discount for any new customer. Look at Comcast, GoDaddy, DirectTV, and the list goes on and on. GoDaddy offers 99 cent domains for the first year. Amazing deal! Beats the $14.95 you are about to pay. So how could they resist? Could you have resisted? What would have kept you loyal? Take care of existing customers/clients! Reward those who have helped get you to where you have gotten.

- For each month you do not communicate with your customers, you lose 10% of your influence with them

On average, a business will lose 50% of its clients every five years, and the cost to replace them is 6 to 7 times more expensive. Think about it, even companies you want to do business with and plan on it. How many times have you visited a website, hit bookmark or put that site in your favorites, because you plan to or want to go back to them to buy from them again, or you do buy from them, but you plan to go back and shop again, but then you don't? Why?

We all have busy lives; we all have fifty million things vying for our attention every day. What is planned, on our calendar, or in front of us are often the things that get our attention. So, the same thing in business. If you are not finding ways to stay in front of your clients face or on their radar often, you are going to lose your influence over them. It won't matter how great your product or service is. It is important to connect and keep in touch often, like they say in personal relationships, to keep the lines of communication open; it works the same for in business as well.

- 67+% of business today is driven by personal referrals and word of mouth

What are you doing to maintain your customer loyalty? What are you doing to attract referrals? You must learn to cultivate and maintain your loyal customers, while at the same time, working to attract new ones. Your customers are people, and people have emotions. The more you can do good and ethical service and provide good products is one thing, but as you keep their hearts and make them feel good, and make them feel important, and make them feel like their "sale" was valued to you, the more they will want to come back to you as well as refer you to others, many times even without you asking.

When you truly connect with your customers, you are making them feel important. You may be the only person in their life who tells and shows them they are important in this world, they are important in your life. Think about how that makes them feel. You could turn a day around for someone. When you do that, you have truly created a relationship. Which is the goal, after all.

REFERRALS – To Ask or Not Ask?

Many people will say, "If you don't ask, you won't get them." While that may be true, at times, I have seen surveys stating, "91% of customers say they would give referrals, but only 11% of people ask for them."

I say, "Don't ask for referrals, deserve them!"

In the early stages of my web and graphic design business, I did not have the money, nor the time to advertise. So I *lived* on 100% referral base, from the beginning. When you live on referrals, you live in the place of "having to provide excellent work. This is something that our society and business world has lost. So, when you live with the mentality as I did (and still do, even though the money flows), "the nice thing about living on referrals was because I did good work, I under-promised and over-delivered; I was competent, diligent, timely and much more."

Most of my clients happily referred me to others. (They still do!) They desire to refer me to others. And, after just a few short years, I found myself making more from home, taking care of our family and children, than my husband was making at his full-time job! Then, within a few more years, I was blessed to about triple that income. I never made a monetary goal for myself, but I made a monetary goal for my tithing to be 5 figures for one year. I was so excited when I hit that goal, and I was able to give that to my God. It was all based from 100% referrals, just doing my business, living my ethics, and obtaining clients who happily referred others to me because I was doing a good job. They knew they would have a good name, by referring me.

What does your name say when someone refers you? Write a list of why you would deserve a referral. What have you done lately? What have you done that is extraordinary? What service did you provide that is out of the park? If I asked you today, "Why would I want to refer my friends, family, and clients to you?" What would your answer be? Today is the perfect day to start deserving those referrals because I know you have it inside of you ready to come out. You are a person worth referring!

How and Where to Start?

Sometimes it is hard to start anything because we don't know how or where. Let me share with you a quick and meaningful tip: Become more intentional about listening to people. Remember you have two ears and one mouth for a reason. Get to know people on a personal level, not just for or in business. Make them feel valued by expressing appreciation with them, and for them throughout the year. You can show them by remembering their special days in their lives, like birthdays anniversary, and other special days of their heart. When you get to know them, you will know the special days of their heart. That comes from true connection, from having a relationship. When you are being who you are on the inside on the outside. Relationships ... based on trust ... happen when we are clear and congruent. When we assure our customers and prospects about the small details and some them the truth in our words and our actions.

"People do business with those they know, like and trust" – Tom Hopkins

Build that know, like and trust relationship with them. Do a good business – provide excellent service or product, whatever it is that you do — do it well. Provide above and beyond customer service. I always say, "Offer 100% to all your customers/clients, but give 150% to each and everyone, including your customer/clients." ☺ Do what you say you are going to do, be where you say you are going to be, etc. Be to someone else the person you need in your life. Watch what happens; when we find a need that must be met, we create a real-life connection. In most cases, these days, people need someone who is real, honest, congruent, and loving. Remember, we are shining so others will see and value our trustworthiness!

When you live a real, congruent and honest life, you will increase your top-of-mind awareness when you connect with them where you can – Facebook, linked in, google plus, email, text or call. And, then up the ante when you occasionally send them a card as well. And, if they are local, invite them to lunch, dinner or coffee every once in a while. It is the perfect occasion just to visit, catch up, and network.

When you find things of interest to someone, send it to them! You might find an email, see an article in a magazine, or something – you think may help them or be useful to them – share it. Look around and listen around in *your* world, for things you can share with others, that they may appreciate.

I took a twist on Tom's phrase, and added to it ☺

"People do business with those they know, like and trust – AND REMEMBER!" – Laurie Delk

Show people you care. It is truly easier than "we" as "human beings" want to make it. It can simply take a few moments a day. It will be the best few moments of your business. Send birthday and anniversary cards. And, also take just an extra few minutes a day on social media to connect with others. It is easy to like and comment on a few posts. Then send a card to someone from an event/post you saw. People post everything, from a lost loved one or the celebration of winning an award, etc. Do you like it when someone "likes" or comments on one of your social media posts? It feels good, right? When you journey through this life side-by-side with someone, imagine the possibilities. And, your journey is even better because you made someone feel important. You allowed someone to know how special they are.

For me, personally, I schedule into my calendar 1 to 3, 15-minute time slots a day on social media. I am bringing my best shot in the smallest amount of time. We can all work smarter. And, keeping it to 15-minutes 1 to 3 times a day is the perfect amount of time to quickly post something and check some other things while connecting with others. It is also the perfect amount of time, so I don't get distracted or sucked into the never-ending hole of social media. It may not be much time, and some days it is none because I am too busy. Be kind to yourself if there is a day when you just can't make it happen. But, don't use excuses either. Business and marketing is easier when you have a plan and stick to it!

Even if I have an extremely busy day planned and being productive means being outside the office all day, I do my best to at least have 1 slot a day; on the same note, remember connecting is not sitting there for hours on end scrolling through posts, not getting anything else done ☺Your schedule and your time is nothing to play around with. Your schedule must include loving on your prospects and customers/clients. Part of your business is providing 150% to your customers/clients! What percentage are you giving to your customers/clients? Do they know how much you care?

"People don't care how much you know, until they know how much you care." — Theodore Roosevelt

The better you become at mastering the relationships in your life – the better you will be at thriving in your personal as well as your business life. Stranger things have happened, right? People can find anything online – any product, any service – and can find anyone with the same or better prices than you. Show why you are different. Show how you are different. The best way to be different is to show how much you care. If you are doing the same thing as your competitors, then it is a scramble to see who wins at the top of the Google search.

Now, when you differentiate and show you care, and stay top of mind with others, those people won't go online to do a search – they will remember you, your name and your business, and then you will no longer be competing with others. ☺ You have established are a relationship. Life is always prettier when you walk it with someone else. When your life is "prettier," you will attract the right people, prospects, and keep the right loyal customers/clients in your life and in your business. Here, in this place, is freedom. Freedom is found when you realize the people in your life see you, like you, and want to show you off. Show off your relationship!

"I've learned that people will forget what you said, will forget what you did, but people will never forget how you made them feel." – Maya Angelou

How do you make people FEEL? How do you want to make people feel? What can you do each day, to enlighten and brighten someone's life around you? Each and every person you come into contact with, you have an amazing opportunity to do something magnificent. What can you do to make them remember you and make them FEEL special? Let them know they ARE special!

With this thought in mind, think about your clients and customers. Pick 1-2 customers/clients a day and find something to share with them, whether it is a card, letter, gift, text, social media message, email, etc. You can touch people in many ways. The key is: it should never be all in one area. Mix it up – find a variety of things and different ways to reach out – listen and search for things that you know they have an interest in.

A cool example here: watch for your customers/clients to post about music. Maybe they are going to see a concert or post a YouTube video with a certain song. Maybe they simply post their favorite song or their wedding song. Search the lyrics of the song. Then, here is where the magic happens. Send them a card … on the inside (or outside) of the card, use some of the lyrics. I guarantee the next time your prospect or customer/client hears that song, they will think of you. If they are thinking of you … they are buying from you! Or better, referring you!

Why does this work? Remember, 80% of the time you should be building relationships with people – keeping in touch for birthday, anniversary, congrats on something special you saw on social media, Happy Thanksgiving/Fall, Merry Christmas, Happy New Year, Happy Ground Hog Day ☺, Happy Valentine's Day, Happy Spring Time, Enjoy Your Summer, Just Thinking About You, Get Well Soon, Happy 4th of July, Teacher Appreciation, Siblings' Day, Whatever Holiday or Occasion you can think of, etc. Remember there is a day for everyone!

80% of the time you are creating a safe environment. An environment when your customers/clients, potentials, and referrals can feel good about opening "a reach out" from you. When they don't have to worry, "what are they selling today?" When they can look forward to getting mail ~ whether it is an email or snail mail! By sending connections 80% of the time, you have created an excitement inside of your customers. One that helps you stand out. How often do you look forward to receiving mail or email from businesses you give your business to? Right, I know. That is why this 80/20 is important to your success. I have clients who can't wait to get their birthday card ... and maybe a birthday brownie every year. They know it is coming. I have created a consistent and safe relationship. A real relationship. This safe environment is important to the TRUST part of the relationship ... and the like part ... and the remembering part! And, that is rewarded.

20% of the time you can market to them – sales promotion, flier, coupon, etc. Not more than this. Otherwise it will become junk/spam mail to them and not valuable. You will be put on their "spam radar," something none of us want, right! As an extra bonus tip: When you are sending the 20%, take advantage of the fact that they will open your email, message, text, card, etc. Ask them for a favor. Ask them to answer a few questions about their experience with you and your business. Ask questions that others in your industry fail to ask. This increases your value as well as increases how valued they feel by you! Then, you can use those questions to create answers ... answers to questions that weren't being asked!

When we are taking time to market during your 20%, still keep your customer/client in mind. Five powerful questions your customer/client and potentials will ask before they reach back out to you?

1. Can I trust you?
2. Will this product/service give me what I need (and want)?
3. If I do this, will it be worth my time, energy, and money?
4. What will others say?
5. Do I really need this?

Let's answer those questions as if you have been using the 80/20 Rule in your business

1. They believe they can trust you because the 80% has developed a relationship with you.

2. They have used your product/service or been referred by someone they trust. They know your work ethics, your values, and morals.

3. Yes, it will be worth my time, energy, and money because I know from experience ... POSITIVE EXPERIENCE!

4. Others will say how smart I am!

5. Yes, I need this ... because it met a need in the past ... a need/want I have again.

We, as business owners, want our customers to get excited when they receive a connection from us. We want them to look forward to seeing that card, that text, that email, or when our phone number pops up on the caller id. They will WANT to see the world through your eyes. See the world you brought to life for them.

When we apply the 80/20 rule in our business, restoration can occur. Is there an industry where you have had a bad example? Or maybe when you think of a specific industry you think of a bad stereotype? When we bring with us into our relationships, into our business, into our connections this fact, "People hear according to their own perceptions, experiences, fears, environment, and style of communication," we can change how people think about the industry we represent.

Quick example of restoration: Not everyone is an ethical business person. Not every business is run with moral principles. There are times when we, as consumers, get burned. Then, we are left with a bad taste in our mouths for that business, and maybe even, the industry as a whole. Think of a bad experience you had. Maybe you were traveling, stopped a hotel. The hotel staff was rude, they overcharged you, the breakfast that was supposed to be provided wasn't, dirty bathroom, and lumpy beds. Yeah, one of those really horrible travel experiences.

Now, let's say, you manage a hotel or maybe manage guest services. You know that some hotels have created a "bad" name for the entire industry. So, what can you do? Restore! Restore! Restore!

Create a list of guests. Inside the list find their check-in's or check-out's dates. You can start sending cards. Send a Happy New Year! Or maybe a welcome to Spring with some tips for spring break travel. Then an Anniversary visit card with a coupon for their next visit. You are creating a relationship. If there is a brokenness … you can bring healing.

While you help others, build friendships, celebrate people's lives and offer amazing, above and beyond service, you will be also, at the same time, building your brand to be a trusted name to use, to share and to remember. You can build friendships and celebrate people's lives through social media, texts, phone calls, in person lunches/coffees, by sending cards for birthdays/thank you/congrats/sympathy and more. I know many of my clients now look for my cards. I have created an excitement around those special days … an excitement that involves me!

Build and create relationships with large networks and numbers of people, who know the service and products you provide, through – Friendships, Celebration, and Service. Be committed to the journey of establishing large networks, even if the road is curvy, bumpy, or foggy. Move ahead. Stay focused. And, when you take the time for others, the road straightens, smooths, and clears! When you focus on friendships, celebrating, and serving ... you have created the road you desire.

Friendships – connect with them on social media like their posts, comment on them. Invite them out to lunch, dinner, coffee (no business, just to chat and get together).

Celebration – when you see something happen in their life (they usually post about it on social media) send them a card or gift, congratulating them, or whatever the occasion they posted about. Make a list of things you celebrate, so you know what to look for. Again, you are being for someone else what you want/need in your own life.

Service – Help where you can with no strings. (Something amazing happens when you go into a situation with a servant heart. A true servant heart. When you don't expect anything in return.) They had a baby? Or the mother is sick? Provide a meal for the family. Drive by their house, lawn need mowed and you know they've had things going on? Do it, or pay someone to do it for them, anonymous. Attend their open house or charity event. Take the time step up when no one asks. It is "easy" to say "yes" when you get asked. You almost feel obligated. When you do things without being asked. That is what means the most. People remember that because that is what an extraordinary relationship is all about — stepping up when some needs it, to notice when someone is struggling, having a bad day, needing a friend and being too scared to ask and telling someone you accept them just the way they are. Remember, like I said earlier … When you serve more than you expect, give more than you get, people become more than people you met.

Look through your contact list, every day, and choose 5-10 people with whom you are going to connect, or reach out, in some way today – no business – just to reach out and connect. Could be as simple as a text, could be a phone call, or an email, could be a greeting card, or taking them out to lunch. It forms a true connection. It forms a real relationship, which so many are looking for. You will meet a need. A need that must be met. You will be remembered for that!

LISTEN to LIFE with KINDESS ears

In your conversations, listen for reasons to celebrate life: congratulations, promotions, marriage, new car, encouragement, new baby, graduation, etc.

When you take the time to speak or connect, find out about something about their week, using FORM (family, occupation, relationship, money). Make mental notes while talking about things so you can send them a card, or even a text or email, or a Facebook message later.

When you show you are listening you are saying 2 things. First, I care. Two, I have opened my heart and found the courage to trust.

Be *THAT* person who celebrates OTHERS! Let that celebration be part of your story!

Recognizing, Listening, and Acting on Promptings

When you receive acts of kindness, send cards! There is always a reason to celebrate! There is always a reason to celebrate and show gratitude. You can teach them what appreciation, with no strings attached, looks like. One of my business partners and I run something called Gratitude Girls. We interview and share the stories of those who have overcome extreme devastation to find and teach other to have gratitude.

When you hear some of these stories, they are inspiring. So inspiring that you realize if they can have gratitude so can you! Show your prospects and customers/clients how to have gratitude and celebrate! We can celebrate the small areas of life. We don't have wait for the big blessings. Think about your neighbor who shoveled your sidewalk; the person who sold you your phone and walked you through setting it up; your mother, for watching the kids so you could have a date; your client who just gave you a referral; the waitress at the restaurant who helped to make your evening more special; or the dry cleaner who made your business suit look professional.

Now, we can celebrate the big events too! Watch your newspapers for wedding announcements, special birthdays, anniversaries, obituaries, and other bits of news where someone might appreciate being remembered.

Church bulletins usually provide information on new babies, baptisms, new members, encouragement, pastor appreciation, get well cards for those who are sick and have missed or in the hospital, sympathy cards. It doesn't always have to be, or just have to be the pastor sending those cards. They would feel more as a church family, as they receive them from others as well.

Newsletters from customers. If they are celebrating or offering something special through their business, take the time to acknowledge that celebration as well as celebrating them. Maybe the newsletter shares a new office address — Congrats. Maybe they are doing a survey of their own customers — WOW, acknowledge their efforts to make a connection.

What are some ways you find information? Make a list. Now, we have eliminated an excuse. You know where to gather information to keep the connection moving forward ... to keep building the relationship.

Relationship Building. My focus. You probably want to know how this relationship building thing has worked for others ... outside of how it has worked for me. Here are a few testimonials, I know you want to read. Read these and take them to heart. See how your business or your life could fit into these examples. See yourself having these same successes. Your success only has the perimeter you give to it.

When you see relationships in their entirety, your vision of business changes. You don't just send the follow up after you meet or the thank you after you get the first round of business. Your vision must include more than the honeymoon phase. Relationships develop deeper when you are consistent, reliable, spontaneous long past the honeymoon phase. To be reliable: To be spontaneous: To be heard: Your voice was designed to be heard!

Testimonial Case Study for simply building Friendships:

Real Estate Broker: Jay McHugh

"In 2008, I took my real estate brokerage from 5 offices and 47 agents, to 14 offices and 300 agents; simply by using a system we call "Random Acts of Cardness.

We are on pace to sell $1 billion of real estate in 2015, a 41% increase in 2 years, thanks to the system we have been using to express gratitude and stay in touch with our clients and other important people."

Testimonial Case Study for Business Store Owner:

Owner, Experimac, Mt Juliet, TN: Scott Maulsby

" At first glance, I was not impressed with Send Out Cards. Then I found myself on the receiving end of a personalized thank you card from a vendor I didn't even do business with. In 20+ years of professional business experience I had never received anything like it. Now Send Out Cards had my attention. I signed up to send cards the next day and a few days later I was a distributor. Almost daily I interact with someone that has received a card from me and it is all we talk about. I can't think of a better way to keep my business in front of past, present and future customers."

Testimonial Case Study for Networking:

Publisher, BestVersionMedia.com: John Sharpe

"Admittedly, at first it didn't register. How could sending cards make such a huge impact?

I met Laurie, and she invited me to a SOC Regional Meeting. That day, the light bulb went on for me! I signed up immediately, and began sending cards to people that I met with. The results that followed were completely unexpected, and astounding! I've been sending cards randomly to business contacts, friends and family, and now realize the pure joy and happiness I'm bringing to the people who receive them.

The system is so easy to use, I can literally send out a customized, 3 panel card, in less than 5 minutes, right from my computer, tablet or phone.

I truly can't imagine growing my business without Send Out Cards. It is the BEST business and personal relationship building tool I possess!"

Testimonial Case Study for Celebrating Others Lives:

Real Estate Broker: Jim McCord

"One of my clients that bought a home last year, is a dentist. He opened a new dental office and it was mentioned in our local paper. I put the article on the front of a card, and sent it to him with a congratulatory note, and a few brownies."

Testimonial Case Study for Saying Thank You:

Non-Profit, Patrick's Everyday Warriors, President: Erin Forte-Froehling

"When someone takes time out of their schedule to volunteer, we — at Patrick's Everyday Warriors — always take the time to say thank you. Yes, we acknowledge them on social media, send them a thank you email, but it is when we go that extra mile and send a card when we see our appreciation is truly acknowledged. Those volunteers are more likely to volunteer again; they desire to help our cause shining a light on pediatric cancer siblings. They even hang up the card (with our logo) as a trophy! Look at what I did! Then, there is the bonus, because the card has our logo on it, free publicity when they hang up their trophy!"

As you meet people, try to connect with them on social media, like and comment on their posts here and there, get their mailing address and their birthday, so you can connect with them outside of social media, share things with them, celebrate with them, and stay top of mind! In a social media driven world, we can more of an impact when we step outside of the "box" called the phone, called the computer, called our idea of society tells us to do.

Joe Girard had a family who needed to be fed. He begged a car dealer to allow him to sell cars for him on a commission only basis, because no one else was hiring at the time that he could find. One finally agreed. Joe Girard was the "World's Greatest Salesman", listed in the Guinness Book of World Records, for 12 years, for selling about 5 cars a day – none of them "fleet sales". Each car sold was one-car-at-a-time.

Now how do you possibly grow a business to the point where you're selling 5 cars a days, one-car-at-a-time?

Well, early in his career, Joe discovered – and utilized – "the Law of 250", which meant to him that for every satisfied, happy, smiling customer that drove off his car lot in a new vehicle, they were going to show off their new purchase to all of their friends – which, on average, would number about 250. One happy, satisfied, smiling customer could open the door to other sales around a new set of 250 prospects. Those are odds that are definitely in your favor!

And, as they told their friends about their new car, Joe Girard's name would come up. Joe simply made the commitment that he would never let that die.

His secret: he built and maintained relationships. He began sending out Thank You cards, Anniversary cards, Birthday cards – any excuse to make certain that he stayed in front of, and top-of-mind with, every one of his satisfied, happy, smiling customers. He would send one card a month, every single month, to anyone he ever met, his prospects and his clients. He created top-of-mind awareness with all those around him. Then whenever the subject of cars was talked about among friends, so would the name of Joe Girard.

Separate yourself from all your other competitors and marketers. Everyone can ask for referrals. You see posts or get emails all day long that resemble this, "Do you know anyone looking to buy or sell a house. Great. Send them my way." (post from a realtor)

Question: Why would you want to refer one of your family members, friends, or customers to that realtor? What have done for you? Do you know them personally? Do you know their work ethic? Or, are they just using the market to their advantage?

Many people knew what Joe Girard did, even the salesmen who worked in the same building. But, they did not want to take the time or expense to do what he did. Therefore, they did not have the sales, nor the income that Joe enjoyed.

Use relationship building consistently and correctly, and it creates a revolution of kindness. And, more importantly, a referral business.

When you want to promote yourself and build your brand and your products or service, you want to talk less about all the great features you, your company or your service/product has. Think about it, your customers could care less "how great you are," right?

You want to focus on the benefits – how can your product or service help them, or what can they do for them. You can talk about and share stories of how others have benefitted, what solutions have been provided, what strategies it helped others with, etc. Sharing how it will help them, and relating with stories that would be similar for them – would make them want your product or service and make them more interested. Remember it is not the "I" and "Me" words. It is about the You and Your words. How we can best serve you, you will receive, your words are heard, etc. The quality of relationships will always be stronger when you share and show others how much you care about them instead of trying to get them to care about you.

SYSTEM: Saves You Significant Time, Energy and Money
Get on board with one amazing support system/team. You want to master the bridge between the high-tech world and the personal-touch side of the world. You can do this by using systems that help you to stay in touch with your

clients, customers, patients, and prospects in personal ways, by using your electronic devices such as: your desktop, laptop, tablet and even your smart phone. We can connect with our customers/clients right from our hands!

When we stay in constant connection with our clients/customers and provide quality work with ethics/morals, we can heal wounds from others in your industry. Not everyone provides quality work. But, you do. Not everyone uses good business ethics or does business with morals. But you do. How do your prospects and clients know? You keep in contact with them. You aren't scared to connect. When you build the right relationship with the right people … you will always maintain the edge above your competitors!

Greeting cards are opened 11 times more than any other piece of mail. Did you read that correctly? Greeting cards are opened 11 times more than any other piece of mail! Who feels like they just found a key to increasing their business, increase their connections with prospects, increase their communication with their customers, their visibility, their credibility, and their sales?!?!

A beauty academy had a business, where members pay a monthly fee to be involved. Sometimes, members' payments would not go through! Whether it was expired card, got a new card, insufficient funds, maxed out, (could be a number of reasons, right?). One test they did, they sent 4 different emails at different times – they realized a 6% success rate of fixing payments with this option. When they sent out a real post card in the mail, it was better. They saw some success. With one mailing, they got a 15% success rate!

Then, they saw a way to do something even different, maybe even way far out there. They sent a greeting card. You know the piece of folded card stock that is placed in an envelope, a name and address is written on the front, and a stamp is stuck to top right-hand corner. Just had to make sure you were clear because knowledge of the greeting card business seems to be lacking. (We place to much focus on what we can do from our gadgets.) The card had a picture of the owner in it, tying the customers to the business even more! Now note, the message in the greeting card was the exact same message as was in the 2nd email! With this option, the company realized a 30% success rate! Remember, greeting cards are opened 11 times more than any other piece of mail. So you can say, "Success is IN the cards!" ☺

A few ways to connect with your Clients, Customers, Patients, Prospects

When someone does business with you, send them a thank you card and/or gift letting them know how much you appreciate their business. Then two weeks later, you might follow that up with a referral card, asking them if they know of anyone else who could benefit from your business. You can do this automatically in the system that I use: SendOutCards.

Keep In Touch with people. Have you ever called someone who you haven't spoken to in a while and then you planned to ask them for a favor or want to tell them about your new business? It's kind of weird, if not wrong, or bad feeling, isn't it? It can even be a business turn-off. This is happening more and more as social media explodes. Have you ever gotten one of those Facebook messages, "Hey friend, I just wanted to let you I am now doing this XYZ business. It is really cool. And, I thought of you." Why did you think of me? Really? Am I supposed to feel great that you are trying to sell me skin care, weight loss products, etc. Do you think I look old? Fat? Need new make-up that bad? There is a disconnect here and most likely, after getting one of these messages, I would not do business with that person. They didn't connect with me. They came right out of the gate selling. They are 100% selling, instead of 80% connecting.

It is important to keep in touch with people on a consistent basis, so you can avoid that problem. When you keep in touch with someone with a card, it is easier then to pick up the phone when you want to talk to them about something.

Share Referrals with others. Find someone who is marketing to the same type of people as you, and send them a card about wanting to share referrals. Offer to endorse their company to your contacts and have them be willing to do the same for you.

Give Referrals to others in business. If you know someone who needs a something, instead of just having them call your business friend, send that friend a card including the contact information of your referral. One really neat thing is your business friend will not throw that card away because it is a great reminder to them of that referral, and you. They, then, will want to give you referrals, more than likely, as well. It is called the law of reciprocation.

Look for ways you can give, watch for ways you can help, look for times when you see someone doing extra – over and above the call of duty for what was required. Send them a card, tell them that you appreciate them.

Thank You For The Referral - It is VERY important to show appreciation to people who take the time to send you referrals. Make sure to send them a card and/or a gift for the referrals that they send you. You reward behavior that you want to be repeated. They did not *have* to send you the referral, right? If you want them to do it again – thank them for it.

Events - If you are speaking at an event, send the person who asked you to speak a card in the mail, letting them know that you appreciate the opportunity. Also, send anyone in the room you just met a "Nice to meet you" card, and you might include on that card, some of the tips you gave at the meeting for them to help remember you. If you attend an event, send the organizer a card thanking them for having the event for you to be able to go and meet and network with others.

Just because you work hard, just because you own your own business, just because provide good service … that does not entitle you to referrals. That does not entitle you to loyal customers. You have to step up, be creative, be different, become "the hostess with mostest" or "the host with the most!" Still doesn't mean you will be entitled, but customers and clients are more likely to see you as deserving!

Mary Kay Ash taught her consultants to write 3 handwritten notes, every night before bed. She said, *"Everyone has an invisible sign hanging from their neck saying 'Make me feel important'. Never forget this message when working with people."*

Tom Hopkins went from making less than $50 per month in real estate, to over 14 million annually within 5 years. He simply decided to write 10 thank you notes, every single day. 99% of his business was by referral within 3 years. Some of his ideas for his notes were – "Thank you for taking time with me on the telephone today; thank you for meeting with me; thank you for your business, thank you for the referral; thank you for the service you provided for me; thank you for your time of you considering to use my service/product: and thank you for using our service/product (one year anniversary)."

The cost of retaining an existing customer, is about 10% of the cost it is to establish a new customer. If you had a 5% improvement in your customer retention, that would equal about 25-85% improvement in profitability. Nurtured customers make about 47%

larger purchases than non-nurtured leads. Reduce your marketing costs, and increase your existing customer up-sells and creates an increase in repeat sales.

The number one reason customers leave to do business elsewhere is perceived indifference 68%. 14% dis-satisfied with your product/service. 9% price competition. 5% leave to buy from a friend. 3% move. 1% die. So that means almost 70% of people left, simply because they did not think you cared! How do you think you could resolve those statistics?

For each month that you do not keep in touch with your clients, you lost 10% of your influence with them.

"We make a living by what we get. We make a life by what we give." ~ Winston Churchill

SALES STATISTICS

48% of sales people never follow up with a prospect

25% of sales people make a 2nd contact and stop

12% of sales people make a 3rd contact and stop

10% of sales people make 4 or more contacts.

2% of sales are made on the 1st contact.

3% of sales are made on the 2nd contact.

5% of sales are made on the 3rd contact.

10% of sales are made on the 4th contact.

80% of sales are made on the $5^{th} - 12^{th}$ contact.

Networking – Collecting Contacts – Do you have a Follow-up plan?

When it comes to networking and your contacts, you need a follow up plan. A plan to follow up! This is where and when most people fail. You can succeed at this moment. You know a lot more people than you think you do. So, there is no way you can remember each and every person in your head, along with their contact information, birthdays, anniversaries, etc. Well, maybe you can. However, I do suggest having a list. It opens you mind to focus on other things. Create your contacts: family, friends, professionals, people who provide services to you, sales people, your Facebook and linked in friends, your cell phone contacts, people you met networking …

Create a list and a plan of activities to capture more contacts: social media, website, email newsletters, blogs, buying leads, direct mail, event marketing, and going to networking events…

When you build relationships with your prospects, many times they will become your customers. Even if they don't become your prospects, you have developed a relationship with them. So if they don't need your service or product, they will know someone who does. Then, what will they do because you have built and established trust? They will send you referrals …

Opportunities to connect: thank you, birthday, holiday, recognition, lifestyle, celebration, wedding, baby arrival, adoption, new pet, marketing, promotions…

Vehicles to connect: Texting; phone calls; emails; social media likes, posts, pictures, events, shares, and personal message; face-to-face meetings; greeting cards…

When you build relationships with your customers, many times they will become your repeat customers, and give you referrals! This is when you will truly see an improved ROI. The connections and relationships will provide joy in your life and business (sales). Combining friendship, joy, business, and sales is what your goal must be. This is called living!

The Power Of Networking

Remember Networking is about connecting or linking to operate interactively! Harvard Business School says the average business person has 250 people in their network. I told you that you knew more people than you thought you did. Now, add all of your connections from social media — crazy amount of people! For the sake of keeping networking stream-lined, let's focus on the 250 contacts. If each one of those connected you to their 250, you'd have 62,500 connections! A well maintained network of about 100 people could lead you to millions of dollars of business over time. It happens when you stay in touch and build those relationships.

Make your list of your top 100 clients. You should know who has brought you the most business, those you frequent your business the most, those who have already been repeat clients, those who have sent you referrals. If you don't know, this is the time to stop right here, and make that list. Yes, right now. I give you permission to take a few moments to make that list and then come right back to finish this book.

Once you have made your list, it is time to find you. Who are you? How are you different? What is cool and creative way to shine and show your unique selling points. Think about this: It may just revolve around who you are a person. I heard this once, "Your brand is who you are 110% of the time because that is when you are authentic. And, authenticity sells!" Authenticity helps you must differentiate yourself from your competition. Differentiating yourself will include following a plan to keep in touch with those 100 clients, consistently every month for one year. Focus on building relationships with the contacts you already have. You already have a relationship with them, why work even harder to build new ones? *Nurtured Relationships equal repeat business as well as referrals!*

As you do meet new people, each time is an opportunity to connect, make a difference, to impact a heart, and to gain a referral. Networking events may scare you or you may find the exhilarating. Either way, as someone who attends networking events and runs networking events on a regular basis, take this advice to heart: Don't be a chicken.

It is okay to be nervous when you walk into a room full of people you don't know. Just do it anyway. Walk in and be yourself. At the same time, don't run around like a chicken with your head cut off shoving business cards and your 30-second commercial at everyone you see. This is being a quantity networker. They are memorable but not for the right reasons. You remember them as "that" person. That person you "will never do business with!"

Connecting and relationships isn't about meeting everyone. Connecting isn't about making the sale right on the spot. Are you carrying your credit card swipe and products with you to you networking events? No, right. You are networking and building relationships because it is about connecting with the right people. When you connect with the right people and form a real, authentic relationship with them, they will connect with those you who need or want the service/product you provide.

Good Networking: Meet more people – add them to your contact list to start keeping in touch. If you can re-connect with a new contact within 48-72 hours of meeting them, they will be more likely to remember you! Remember the saying, "strike while the iron is hot." When it comes to networking, "Connect while you are still on their minds."

Be a quality networking networker! What does that mean? Focus on your strengths. If you are an introvert, you are most likely a good listener. Take the take time to truly listen. Take notes on business cards so you remember how to make your follow up unique (not generic). When you are unique you are

MEMORABLE! If you are more of an extrovert, use that to your advantage. You can step into conversations and introduce yourself. You can talk to anyone about anything. As an extrovert, you may need to remember to ask the person quality questions. Real questions. And, take notes.

Do you remember people you met one time and now have their business card? Probably not everyone you meet. Plus, this also shows you enjoyed meeting them! Making them feel good, important, and loved. In turn, they will develop feelings for you. They may just "like" you and develop a "trust" for you. We do business, again, with those we like and trust and remember!

Be known as the authentic connector – connect people together who need and can use each other. Think of yourself as a puzzle connector. This simple action will build your brand and build your credibility. You are being useful. This is so important in being remembered. We remember those who do things for us! When you have an authentic brand and honestly want people to connect, something spectacular happens. You have written a page or two or even a chapter in your story!

Appreciation Rocks and Rules - Appreciate people by keeping in touch: nice-to-meet you cards, phone calls, gifts, birthday, anniversary, one-on-one networking lunches, send them referrals...

Let's get southern for a moment. Not sure your thoughts or the embedded stereotypes in your mind about NASCAR. If you need a lesson in marketing, watch NASCAR. They are on the right track and can steer you in the right direction. Customer/driver loyalty amazes me.

Each driver truly appreciate his/her sponsors, and they thank their sponsors each chance they have. This creates a memorable loyalty for the fans. If you were a Jeff Gordon fan, most likely you didn't drink coke. Why? Pepsi was his main sponsor. And, if you did like Jeff and knew Jeff owned part of Jimmy Johnson's car ... you weren't buying at Home Depot for you home improvement needs. Yeah ... you got it, Lowe's is one of Jimmy's main sponsors.

For NASCAR fans it has become instinct because of the consistency of the driver's gratitude.

Most people are doing the same thing every day without achieving the results they want, without seeing their goals come to fruition, without living the life they truly desire. These people are insane, especially when there is a system that works.

"Insanity – Doing the same thing, over and over again, expecting different results" – Albert Einstein

Are you doing the same things in your business expecting different results? An anchor can't do its job unless it is tied to a rope, which is tied to the boat. A plan will never work unless we put it into action and do it consistently.

So, I challenge you to try relationship marketing into action for twelve months. For twelve months, make your list of contacts, include their special days (birthdays, anniversaries, etc). Consistently, connect with them on social media. Then, set your goals.

Create realistic goals because you don't want to feel overwhelmed or spread yourself too thin. On the other hand, it is okay to get out of your comfort zones. The only way to grow is to do something you have never done! How many contacts do you want to connect with each day? How much time can you afford to spend on social media — liking and commenting, sharing posts, doing what you can to make people feel important, and capturing the important aspects of your contacts' lives. How many texts will you send each day? And, when it comes to truly making your contacts feel special … remember the perfect cards to send to them. Nothing else says love these days like mailbox love. Send away!

With your goals, make sure they are clear and specific.   Choose a "magic" number — one that know you can accomplish and at the same time are doing more than you were doing! Once your goals are set, get organized. Being organized helps us know when and if we are accomplished everything we need to accomplish while knowing how much time we are using.

Prepare your calendar. When is the best time to connect? When can you do it and be constant the most easily.

As you set out in the morning or afternoon or evening to connect with your customers/clients, review your notes and business cards. Did you ask enough quality questions? Ask yourself when you reach out, "if you were them, why would they care about you reaching out."

Your follow up and consistent connection is the eye contact of conversations. When you are having an in-person conversation, how do you feel if the person won't make eye-contact with you? You are less likely to trust them, right? Well, when it comes to follow up and your time, those days you feel like you just can't do it anymore, remember this, consistent follow up is building trust. If you want to be trusted enough for that referral, make your follow up count! Make it consistent! You are looking at them in the eye!

Other doubt issues could arise. The potential customers said, "I already have a person who does what you do." SEND that email. SEND that text. SEND that Facebook message. SEND that card anyway! You never know if they may ever need your service/product or who they might refer because you took the time to connect and connect consistently!

Be patient with your follow up during this 12-month challenge. A quality relationship isn't formed overnight. It takes time. It is okay if it doesn't come natural at first. What gives us the most fulfilling success ... comes when we "work" toward a goal. It feels so good when we accomplish that goal.

When the relationship is real, the next steps are easier, and they move faster. A real relationship avoids shameless self-promotion and is truly useful to the other person involved. Connection is EVERYTHING!

Remember to connect with me on social media, and at my website www.LaurieDelk.me and share your testimonials with me! I look forward to connecting with you and hearing about your 12-month challenge.

I look forward to building a relationship with you. For you never know, who I might be able to refer your way! What are you waiting for? And, of course, I am ready to send some mailbox love.

www.ingramcontent.com/pod-product-compliance
Lightning Source LLC
Chambersburg PA
CBHW060407190526
45169CB00002B/787